# BLARNEY
## through the mists of time

by
DR. SEAN PETTIT
University College, Cork

Illustrations by
GLADYS LEECH

Published by Blarney Castle Estate

*Printed in Ireland*

Books by the same author available at Blarney Castle
Gift Shop and by mail order:
The Streets of Cork
My City by the Lee

© Copyright 1989  Sean F. Pettit

*Printed by Litho Press Co. Midleton Co. Cork*

## Introduction

To visit Blarney Castle is to step back in time, and to feel the enchantment of a long and heroic past. Here is one of the great historical sites of Ireland and a tourist attraction that is renowned throughout the world. Yet the visitor will find that the whole atmosphere is refreshingly relaxed, without the bother of queues or harassment of any kind. Blarney is a tranquil place, and something of the peace and beauty of its countryside hangs in the air. There is an old Irish saying that "when God made time he made plenty of it." Certainly, there is plenty of time in Blarney and plenty of space in which to spend it with interest and enjoyment.

Of course, the great centrepiece is Blarney Castle itself and the ritual of Kissing the Blarney Stone. Therein lies the legend and all its romantic associations. But there is much more to be seen and enjoyed. The natural beauty of the 400 acres of parkland and avenues, the profusion of splendid trees, some as old as a thousand years, the rich bird life, the pre-historic rocks in the Rock Close, and the period charm of the interior of Blarney Castle House, all of these claim the attention of the visitor. And Blarney village itself has its own intimate charm. A full morning or afternoon at Blarney will give a unique insight into the splendour of Ireland's heritage of history and natural beauty.

This booklet is designed to help the visitor to appreciate the fascinating story of Blarney Castle and its surroundings from its origins down to the present time. Part One gives the historical development. This is not, however, a mere catalogue of dates and battles, but rather a tapestry of human life and action, weaving together the many strands that went into the making of an Irish castle and an Irish village. Part Two provides a compact guide to the Castle and its surroundings, with each entry having a number that corresponds with the signpost on the spot. Many of the briefer references in Part Two will have been more fully explained in Part One.

In expressing my thanks to Mr. Charles Colthurst for the invitation to write this booklet, I also acknowledge the helpful background information supplied by the owner of the Blarney Castle estate, Sir Richard La Touche Colthurst Bart. Much valuable assistance has been given by Mr. Ignatius Buckley, who has given a lifetime of service to tourism in the Cork region, while my wife, Aruba, has helped me to become more familiar with site locations. The staff in the Cork Room of the Cork City Library gave a service that reflected their usual courtesy and efficiency as I pursued my research. I hope that this little book will give the reader a happy reflection of a lovely place.

# PART ONE

## SETTING THE SCENE AT BLARNEY

Blarney Castle is part of the nostalgia of Ireland as it stands there looking so silent and so strong, framed by gentle hills and clumps of tall trees that have weathered the storms of a thousand years. All of us are touched in our imaginations by the sight of an ancient ruin, be it castle or abbey or great house; it evokes a certain sense of romance, a feeling of reverence for times past. We have an instinct to explore it and to catch some fleeting glimpse of the people whose voices were heard there as they built it and lived in it. All of those emotions are evoked by Blarney Castle. Even in a country so profusely dotted by ancient ruins as Ireland is, the massive square tower at Blarney is unique as a fortress dating back to the fifteenth century. In the early centuries of its glory it witnessed the triumph and the tumult of Irish chiefs, with knights in suits of armour on their prancing horses in the castle grounds, and ladies elegantly busy with embroidery, and the shouts of hilarity from the Banqueting Hall as guests were entertained at an evening feast with whiskey and roast pig. There were more sombre times, too, when enemy armies, both Irish and English, besieged the Castle and the air was filled with the clash of arms and the cries of the wounded. By the year 1700 Blarney

Castle's great days as an Irish fortress had gone forever. People no longer came to fight or to feast.

By 1800, however, the first trickle of visitors was coming to this ancient place to do one of the loveliest things that people do at any time or any place, to bestow a kiss. The legend of Kissing the Blarney Stone was born, with all its associations of romance, superstition and fun. As the last century progressed, Blarney Castle acquired a worldwide reputation and the trickle of visitors became a throng of tourists. To-day the Castle is probably the best-known and the most photographed building in the whole of Ireland. Perhaps its most ardent admirers come from America to find in it something of the very essence of old Ireland, a romantic ruin, the memories of ancient glory, the charm of its setting amid the fresh green fields, and the allure of "a touch of the Blarney." The magic never fails, and all who Kiss the Blarney Stone can be assured of being endowed with the eloquence of Irish talk, soft, persuasive, with just a nice touch of flattery and a twinkle in the eye. The visitor to Ireland will find this kind of talk not only at Blarney but everywhere, down a country road, at a street corner, over a farmyard gate and around the fire in a pub. People still have time to talk in Ireland.

Having explored the Castle and performed the ritual of Kissing the Blarney Stone, the visitor still has much more to enjoy. The Rock

Close contains a collection of fascinating boulders and passages dating back to prehistoric times, including the Witch's Kitchen and the Wishing Steps, while a fine selection of ancient trees is offset by recent landscape gardening and rustic bridges over the River Blarney. In this secluded spot, so tranquil and timeless, the visitor will feel at peace with the world. Here, too, a gentleman might use his new-found eloquence to speak soft words to a lady! The stroll across the meadow to the modern Blarney Castle House is rewarded by the sight of some splendid trees and the possibility of a glimpse of the herd of one hundred deer. A tour of the House is a journey back to the age of elegance, with furniture and fittings displaying the craftsmanship and sense of taste of the great period houses of Ireland and Europe.

If Blarney Castle is the jewel in the crown, the village of Blarney has a charm and interest of its own. it is quite literally an outcrop of the Castle, and is one of the finest examples in Ireland of what is known as an estate village or town. In the second half of the eighteenth century a development was taking place in Britain and Europe whereby a progressive landlord created a model village adjacent to his estate, supplying the basic needs for a local industry and housing for the workers and their families. Such was the origin of Blarney village. In 1765 James St. John Jeffereys, whose family had bought the

Blarney Estate in 1703, set about making a model estate village. With remarkable foresight and energy, and entirely at his own expense, he proceeded to lay out the present village square and to group houses for the workmen on three sides of it, with a long narrow garden behind each house. Shrewdly making use of a natural amenity, he built watermills to entice industry. His projections were successful and soon Blarney was a thriving industrial settlement. Pride of place went to the Blarney Woollen Mills, owned by Messrs Martin Mahony. Blarney tweed won a world reputation for excellence and was displayed in the fashion houses of London, Paris and New York. The Mills employed 700 workers in a series of fine stone buildings still to be admired. Sadly, the enterprise was adversely affected by external economic problems and ceased operations in 1975. However, there is life and work once again at Blarney Woollen Mills where an imaginative adaptation of the old buildings has created a tourist centre with a craft ship, restaurant and the manufacture of high quality woollen garments which find a world-wide market.

Such, then, is the Blarney scene. A gracious place made historic by Blarney Castle and the fine expanse of the parklands of the Blarney Castle Estate with the elegance of its period House. The village, too, adds its own quaint charm and its long tradition of craftsman ship. That leads to one obvious question: how did it happen that in this quiet place of gentle hills and small streams so much history and romance and labour came to be blended?

## THE MAKING OF BLARNEY CASTLE

One of the many definitions of history is that it is "a great story nobly told." Certainly, Blarney Castle and its surroundings embrace the elements of greatness as they touch people and places. The site emerges from the mists of history as the ancestral stronghold of one of the most powerful of the ancient clans of Ireland, the MacCarthys. Because of the vastness of their estates and the prowess of their arms they had achieved the distinction of being recognised as Kings of Munster by the lesser Irish chiefs, Munster being the most southerly of the four provinces of Ireland. Tracing their ancestry back to a chieftain who was converted to Christianity by St. Patrick, the MacCarthys produced many warriors who left their mark on time and place, such as Cormac MacCarthy who built the famous Cormac's Chapel on the Rock of Cashel, 1127 to 1134. Yet another MacCarthy was prominently involved in one of the major turning-points of Irish history, the coming of the Normans from England in 1169. Having secured domination over that country with their victory at the Battle of Hastings, 1066, it was inevitable that they would turn their eyes to the sister isle. Their

intention was sanctified by a Bull
from Pope Adrian IV authorising the
Norman King of England, Henry II,
to correct alleged abuses in the
Church in Ireland. After some initial
bloody encounters, the majority of
the Irish chiefs recognised Henry
as their overlord. Among those to
do so was Dermod MacCarthy, King
of Munster. One immediate result
was that the city of Cork was
transformed into a walled medieval
city in the European pattern
favoured by the Normans. Always
generous patrons of the Church,
Tracton Abbey near Carrigaline, Co.
Cork, and Muckross Abbey at
Killarney were built by MacCarthy
chieftains.

    Eventually, they selected
Blarney as the site of their major
Munster fortress. It is believed that
as early as the tenth century there
was a wooden hunting lodge on the
site. This was followed some time
later by a small stone structure,
only to be demolished in 1446 when
the building of the existing massive
structure was begun. The builder
was one of the more eminent of the
MacCarthy chieftains, Dermot, King
of Munster. The calibre of the man
can be inferred from the title given
him in the Irish language by his
contemporaries, Dermot Laidir,
Dermot the Strong. Born in 1411 he
lived a long life until he was killed in
1494. An earlier historian has
described him graciously as "a
prince of distinguished valour, and
a munificent patron of the church,
of art and of learning." He was
married to Mary, the daughter of

Edmond Fitzmaurice, the ninth Lord of Kerry. In the family tradition he built Kilcrea Abbey for the Franciscans, and there the old warrior was finally laid to rest and his tomb may be seen amid the ruins.

The monumental task of building Blarney Castle was the work of many hands and many years. It must be realised that what is left as present is known as the keep, or chief fortress residence. In its original state the existing keep was set in an enclosed area of about eight acres of land, with a perimeter wall and a series of small guardtowers. The Castle was, in fact, a miniature walled town. Moreover, it was self-sufficient as regards all essential supplies and services, because the whole fundamental point about any castle in Ireland or Europe was that it should provide safety and the necessities of life for that one supreme eventuality for which it was designed, the time of attack or the time of siege. Quite literally, a castle was a defence machine. Blarney Castle was not built as a tourist attraction, but rather as a matter of life and death. But why was it necessary to take such elaborate precautions against attack, and who were the likely attackers? In the centuries between 1100 and 1600 European countries did not have standing national armies or police forces; local lords had the responsibility of defending themselves and their territory and tenants. Furthermore, fighting was the honourable profession of a knight or gentleman, the one way of life for which he was trained since boyhood. Land had to be snatched from neighbouring chiefs, insults had to be avenged, family feuds had to be settled. Anyway, there was little else to occupy a gentleman except to play chess! In such uncertain and hazardous times the fortified castle emerged as a necessity. The Norman were expert castle builders and it was they who introduced the technique to Ireland after their arrival in 1169. Blarney Castle and its estate would have catered not only for the immediate MacCarthy family but for a whole retinue of knights and retainers; ranged around it were the dairy, the buttery, the blacksmith's forge, the stables for the horses, outhouses for pigs and poultry, and the mill for grinding corn. Safety, strength, durability, these were the prime considerations in the making of Blarney Castle; such modern demands as heating, light, ease of access from one apartment to another, were nowhere in the picture. Even in times of peace life was something of an endurance test. Though Dermot the Strong lived to a ripe old age, it must be remembered that in those times the average life expectation was fifty years of age.

## "A TOUCH OF THE BLARNEY"

The MacCarthy's of Blarney Castle followed the usual pattern of war and peace between their Irish neighbours and their English overlords. Queen Elizabeth I, however, wished to tighten the screw on the Irish chiefs by demanding that they agree to possess their lands under legal tenure from her. Cormac Teige MacCarthy, Lord of Blarney, had no intention of submitting to the Queen's demand, yet as a shrewd politician he made sure to conceal his plan from her. Skilled in subtle diplomacy, he answered every demand from the Queen by a letter protesting his undying loyalty and making flattering references to the person of her Most Gracious Majesty. On the receipt of yet another such letter, Queen Elizabeth lost her royal composure and shouted in rage "This is all Blarney, he never means what he says, he never does what he promises." And so the word "blarney" slipped into the English language, being defined at first as "persuasive talk designed to deceive but not to cause offence." Words, like fashions, undergo a change of emphasis, and by the early years of the last century "blarney" had become an endearing description for a fine flow of eloquence with just a touch of good-humoured exaggeration.

In the ebb and flow of harsh military campaigns and political upheavals that made the century from 1600 to 1700 such a dark one in Irish history, the MacCarthys of Blarney Castle artfully sidestepped from one side to the other in a desperate bid to survive. When a large Spanish force landed at Kinsale, Co. Cork, in 1601, in support of the national Irish chiefs, Hugh O'Neill and Hugh O'Donnell, the MacCarthys were on the side of the English. Yet when Oliver Cromwell brought fire and the sword to Ireland, the MacCarthys stoutly fought in the Irish cause and suffered dearly for doing so. A major technological development in the methods of warfare signalled the end of the era of castles as impregnable fortresses, namely the invention of cannon. With this formidable weapon the attacker could smash breaches in the thick castle walls and could do so from a distance. The *traditional weapons* of the defenders of castles, bows and arrows, spears, swords, boiling water and red-hot pitch, were no match for the heavy long-range cannons. And so, the whole strategy of warfare underwent a dramatic and permanent change, and the long era of castle-building came to an end, not only in Ireland but throughout Europe. Blarney Castle felt the devastating effect of the new weapon in 1646 when a Cromwellian army under Lord Broghill besieged it and took possession. However, with the Restoration of King Charles II in England,m the MacCarthys were back in Blarney Castle by the month of May, 1661, under the head of the clan, Lord Muskerry, bearing a title that had been earlier conferred on the Lord of Blarney. At this point the business of the MacCarthy family name becomes somewhat confusing, because not only was Lord Muskerry restored to Blarney Castle by King Charles but he was elevated to the title of the Earl of Clancarty.

## THE END OF AN ERA FOR BLARNEY CASTLE

By whatever name they might call themselves, the MacCarthys of Blarney were soon to be caught up in a final and fatal act in the drama of Anglo-Irish politics. King James II of England was forced to relinquish his throne because of his open support for the Catholic Church, and the Dutch Protestant prince, William of Orange, became the new king. The stage was now set for a classic confrontation between the two major religious traditions, and Ireland became the battleground for the type of bitter religious war that had already devastated so much of Europe. The two superpowers, England and France, each had a finger in the Irish pie. Assured of the support of the majority of the Catholic Irish chiefs, King James landed at Kinsale, Co. Cork, on the 12th March, 1689, and was welcomed into Cork city by the senior Irish lord, the Earl of Clancarty from Blarney Castle. King Louis of France sent an army to support James, while the forces of William of Orange had a large Dutch contingent. William was victorious at the Battle of the Boyne. It was the end of the political power of the

ancestral Irish chiefs. And the
MacCarthys were forced to leave
Blarney Castle, never to return. In
accordance with the old proverb, "to
the victor go the spoils", the lands
of all who supported King James
were confiscated, while an Irish
army of over 10,000 men were
allowed to sail into exile from Cork
under the command of the Irish
hero, Patrick Sarsfield. As the Irish
Brigades, these men distinguished
themselves by their valour in the
armies of France and Spain. With
an English government annual
pension of £300 a year, the Earl of
Clancarty lived out his days in exile
and died at Hamburg. And so the
sun had set on the great days of
Blarney Castle as a fortress and as
the ancestral residence of the
MacCarthys, Kings of Munster,
Lords of Blarney, Lords of Muskerry
and Earls of Clancarty.

## AN OVERNIGHT GUEST AT BLARNEY CASTLE ABOUT 1615

While the drama of high politics and
bloody battles went on sporadically
in the world outside, Blarney Castle
witnessed all the everyday routine
of an Irish chief, his family and
retainers. People woke in the
mornings to see shafts of sunlight
slanting in through the slit windows,
meals were cooked and eaten,
there was gossip and laughter and
tears, children played, and gallant
knights fell in love with young ladies
dressed in the very latest Flanders
cloth. And in the evening the lord
sat at the head of the great long

table in the Banqueting Hall to preside over a convivial feast of roast meats and Spanish wine, while his personal bard plucked his harp and sang songs glorifying the ancestral prowess of the MacCarthys. An over-night guest at an Irish Castle early in the seventeenth century has left an eye-witness account of his experience, and in broad terms it is applicable to Blarney Castle:

"The Hall is the uppermost room, let us go up, you shall not come down agayne till tomorrow. Take no care of your horses, they shall be sessed among the tenants. The lady of the house meets you with her trayne. Salutations past, you shall be presented with all the drinks of the house. First the ordinary beere, then sacke, then olde ale. The lady tasted it, you must not refuse it. The fyre is prepared in the middle of the hall, where you may sollace yourself till supper time. You shall not want sacke or tobacco. By this time the table is spread and plentifully furnished with a variety of meats, but ill cooked and without sauce. They feast together with great jollity and healths (toasts) around. Towards the middle of the supper the harper begins to tune and singeth Irish rhymes of ancient making. Supper ended, it is your liberty to sit up or depart to your Lodging, you shall have company in both kind. In the morning there will be brought to you a cup of aquavitae (Irish Whiskey), it is a very whole some drink, and natural to digest the crudities of Irish feeding. You may drink a naggin without offence. Breakfast is but the repetition of supper." And so refreshed with his whiskey and full Irish breakfast, the guest at Blarney Castle would be saddled up on his horse to ride off into the crisp morning air.

The MacCarthys were noted as generous patrons of Irish culture, and the Bardic School at Blarney attracted scholars from all over Munster. These Schools were a feature of Irish life throughout the Middle Ages and down to the early seventeenth century, maintaining that tradition of scholarship which in earlier centuries had won for Ireland the title of the "Island of Saints and Scholars." The scholars were an elite class of young men who devoted many years to the study of Irish literature and law, in addition to the Latin and Greek studies which formed the core of the curriculum in the European universities. By about 1600 Blarney had become well known as the seat of a Court of Poetry where poets gathered on festive occasions to read their compositions, many of which have survived in the original Irish form and in English translations. There was always a bard in residence at Blarney Castle, serving the MacCarthy clan as poet, historian and musician. The last in the long line of learned men was Tadhg O Duinnin, one of whose Irish verses contains the line "My craft being withered with the change of law in Ireland."

## MAKING A MODEL VILLAGE AT BLARNEY

History is about change, and out of change comes new life. With the defeat of the Irish cause at the Battle of the Boyne, 1690, the estates of the native chiefs were confiscated by the State and put up for auction. In 1702 the Blarney property was advertised for sale as follows: "Blarney with the Village, Castle, Mills, Customs, and all lands and the park thereto belonging, containing 1401 acres." It had three owners within a short space of time, first the Hollow Sword Blades Company of London, then Sir Richard Payne, but by 1703 it had been bought by Sir James Jefferyes Governor of Cork, in whose family and descendants through intermarriage it has remained ever since. Sir James had seen service in the army of the King of Sweden, and he brought his Swedish wife to Blarney Castle. It was his grandson, James St. John Jefferyes, who distinguished himself and enriched Blarney by embarking on a remarkable enterprise that brought good taste, commercial development and prosperity to the people of the village. James Jefferyes was in the best tradition of what is known as an "improving landlord", bringing progressive plans to his tenants. From 1765 onwards his plans developed with foresight and energy, and Blarney village became an outcrop of Blarney Castle. It was the age of elegance in Europe, and the fashion was that great estate owners were laying out model settlements adjacent to their castles or period houses. Good taste in design went hand in hand with the encouragement new ideas to transform Blarney into a model estate village, one of the finest of its kind in Ireland. In doing so he shrewdly took advantage of the natural amenity of fast-flowing streams to erect water-mills to entice industry into the area. The village is blessed by nature with three small rivers, the Shournagh, the Martin, the Blarney, with a good flow of water and a steep fall from the surrounding hills. The prosperity of Blarney was made of water, a prosperity that was to last for two centuries. Following the principle of good design James Jefferyes laid out the existing village green, and on three sides around he built ninety neat houses for the workers with long narrow gardens behind. A small church was erected on the slope overlooking the village. A plan of the village dating from that period shows the tasteful design, together with the house plots and the names of occupants. In all the landlord built thirteen mills in the locality, and industries flourished in the categories of linen, bleaching, paper-making, flour, dyewood and iron works. The new Blarney attracted visitors not just to see the Castle but to see the great waterwheels turning and to note the prosperity of the men, women and children who worked and lived locally.

One such visitor was Arthur Young, and from his book, "A Tour of Ireland, 1780", there comes one of the most fascinating eye-witness accounts of social life in Ireland in the closing decades of the eighteenth century. Young was an Englishman who gave himself the lifelong mission of promoting improved agriculture, and in pursuit of that cause he travelled through most of Britain, Ireland and many parts of Europe. He came to Ireland to observe and encourage, and being a man of enormous curiosity and acute observation his journal is a masterly portrait of everyday life in Ireland. He had a particular interest in turnips, and when he saw a good crop in a field at Coolmore estate in Co. Cork, he quivered with delight. He dined in the great houses and poked his head into the thatched cabins of the peasants; he went down every boreen and peered over every fence. In 1779 he came to Blarney and this is what he saw: "September 15th to Blarney Castle, S.J. Jefferyes Esq., of whose great works in building a town at Blarney I cannot give so particular an account as he and his family were on the point of setting out for France. I found that in 1765 when Mr. Jefferyes began to build this town it consisted only of two or three mud cabins; there are now ninety houses. He first established the line manufactory, building a bleach mill and houses for weavers, and letting them to manufacturers from Corke, who have been so successful in their work as to find it necessary to have larger and more numerous edifices . . . diapers, sheeting, ticking, and linens and cottons of all sorts are printed here, for common use and furniture. These several branches of the trade employ above three hundred hands." The account went on to note the woollen mill, the stocking mill, the blade mill for grinding edged tools, and the paper mill. Such was the extent and quality of the landlord's development that he was given a grant from the Royal Dublin Society to promote it. Nor did the observant Young miss the improvements at Blarney Castle: "Mr. Jefferyes, besides the above establishments, has very much improved Blarney Castle and its environs. He has formed an extensive ornamental ground which is laid out with considerable taste. An extensive plantation surrounds a large piece of water, and walks lead through the whole. There are several very pretty sequestered spots where covered benches are placed." The "ornamental ground" is the Rock Close which to-day's tourists find so attractive, and the whole description dispels any notion that environmental improvement is somehow a creation of recent times. Well pleased with his Blarney trip, the worthy Arthur Young took off to visit a period house at Dunkettle on the outskirts of Cork city.

There was a general economic depression in Britain and Ireland after the Napoleonic Wars from 1815 to 1820, and a visitor to

Blarney noted in the latter year that the roofs were off most of the houses and corn was growing in the village green. But the village received a new lease of life in 1824 when Martin Mahony established the Blarney Woollen Mills, a step that was to bring prosperity and world fame to the village, and that was to last until 1975. The Woollen Mills became synonymous with Blarney, and in time the lives of every man, woman and child revolved around the great enterprise. By 1900 there were eight hundred workers employed, and Blarney tweed was in the fashion shops of London, Paris and New York. Fathers and sons and daughters worked in the Mill generation after generation, and the factory hooter told the village that it was time for lunch. Production was especially heavy during the 1914-1918 War in supplying uniforms to the British forces, and again during the last war in making uniforms for the Irish army. But by the early 1970s the signs of warning were beginning to show. There was competition from imported products from Asia, Irish wage levels were rising, while the social change to wearing more informal clothes led to a decrease in the demand for traditional fine tweeds. The closure of the Blarney Woollen Mills marked the end of a whole way of life for the local community. Fortunately, the fine range of stone buildings never suffered the indignity of decay; in an imaginative programme of adaptation the whole complex has been developed into a very attractive tourist centre, with hotel, gift shop and the manufacture of high quality fashion garments which find a ready worldwide market. For those interested in industrial archaeology a visit to the ruins of the old Monard Valley Iron Mills, about two miles distant, will have much to offer. Established in 1790 by the Beale family, it made agricultural implements, and was latterly owned by the well-known hardware merchants of Cork, Messrs Scott. The burning of their city premises in 1960 led to the closure of the Monard Mills. To-day the cascading waterfall alone disturbs the silence amid the tall trees, and the massive iron waterwheel still stands in its original position.

## THE BIRTH OF A LEGEND: KISSING THE BLARNEY STONE

The world comes to Blarney to Kiss the Stone and to take away a touch of Irish magic. The origin of the Blarney Stone is lost in the mists of antiquity; it may have been brought back from the Crusades, or it may be the portion of the royal Stone of Scone which Robert Bruce of Scotland gave to Cormac MacCarthy, King of Munster, in gratitude for the Irish army of four thousand men which was sent to help him at the Battle of Bannockburn in 1314. Whatever its origins, ti has woven around itself a unique tradition of legend and romance, a certain innocent belief in magic powers, all made harmless and human by the laughter excited as the ritual of kissing the Blarney Stone follows its traditional pattern. Every day in the year people come from the four quarters of the world to perform that ritual, and they go away feeling that they have had the experience of a lifetime. Blarney makes the world feel relaxed. As has been stated, the use of the word "blarney" goes back to Elizabethan times, but the public ritual of Kissing the Stone seems to date from the development of the Blarney Castle Estate by the Jefferyes family in the late eighteenth century. A rather unflattering reference to the proceedings at the top of Blarney Castle comes from the French Consul in Dublin, Charles Etienne Coquebert de Montbret, who in 1789 set out on a tour of the country. Giving an extremely detailed account of the streets of Cork and of the life that was lived in them, he made reference to "Blarney Castle on the top of which is a large stone that visitors who climb up are made to kiss, with a promise that in so doing they will gain the privilege of telling lies for seven years." This audacious allegation could only have been made by a man with no magic in his soul!

    The attraction of Blarney was greatly boosted by the visit of Sir Walter Scott in August, 1825. His Waverley Novels enjoyed an enormous popularity throughout the English-speaking world, making them the first best-sellers. Both the

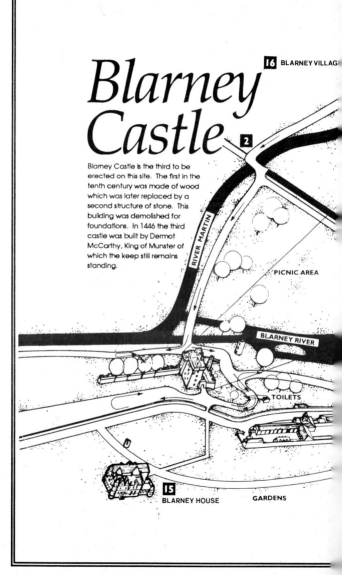

# Blarney Castle

**16** BLARNEY VILLAGE

**2**

Blarney Castle is the third to be erected on this site. The first in the tenth century was made of wood which was later replaced by a second structure of stone. This building was demolished for foundations. In 1446 the third castle was built by Dermot McCarthy, King of Munster of which the keep still remains standing.

RIVER MARTIN

PICNIC AREA

BLARNEY RIVER

TOILETS

**15** BLARNEY HOUSE

GARDENS

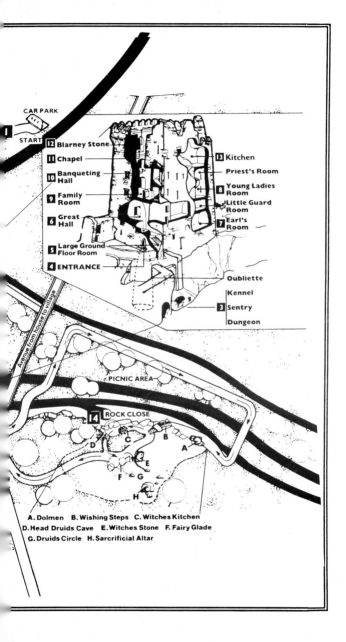

author and his books were especially favoured in Ireland where readers had a ready sympathy with the heroic tales of chivalry and romance in the Highlands of Scotland. Scott had been invited to Ireland by his close friend, Tom Moore, whose "Irish Melodies" will forever be treasured as expressions of the sweetness and the sadness of Irish life. The great man of letters was accompanied by Maria Edgeworth, the noted lady author, and his son-in-law, J.G. Lockhart, who was later to write the classic biography of Scott. A quotation from that book best describes the episode in question:

"Having crossed the hills from Killarney to Cork, where a repetition of the Dublin in reception awaited him — corporation honours, deputations of the literary and scientific societies — he gave a couple of days to the hospitality of this flourishing town, and the beautiful scenery of the Lee; not forgetting an excursion to the groves of Blarney, among whose shades we had a right mirthful picnic. Sir Walter scrambled up to the top of the castle and kissed, with due faith and devotion, the famous Blarney Stone." Scott's visit to Cork came at a time when the city was enjoying a rich cultural life, fashioned by a circle of talented and articulate poets, painters, sculptors and historians, some from very humble homes, but all enjoying high public prestige and the patronage of the "merchant princes". Among them were Daniel

Maclise whose paintings adorn the National Gallery in Dublin and the House of Lords in London, the sculptor, John Hogan, probably the finest Ireland has produced, the writer, Thomas Crofton Croker, and the archaeologist, Father Matt Horgan, from the parish of Waterloo beside Blarney. They created a society of wit and wine, made human by a certain amount of elegant nonsense. One of them, Richard Millikin, had earlier composed simple verses celebrating "The Groves of Blarney":

> "The groves of Blarney,
> They look so charming,
> Down by the purlings
> Of sweet silent brooks,
> All decked by posies
> That spontaneous grow there,
> Planted in order
> In the rocky nooks".

A final verse was added to this poem by another celebrated writer, Francis Sylvester Mahony, and this verse is regarded as the most perfect expression of the powers conferred by Kissing the Blarney Stone. Mahony, writing under the pen name of "Father Prout" was himself a priest who took up a literary career in London and Paris, and counted among his friends Charles Dickens and Thackeray. His poem, "The Bells of Shandon", is the folk anthem of his native Cork. The following lines reveal the secrets of Blarney eloquence:

> "There is a stone there,
> That whoever kisses,

Oh! he never misses
To grow eloquent.
Tis he may clamber
To a lady's chamber,
Or become a member
Of parliament.
A clever spouter
He'll sure turn out, or
An out-and-outer
To be let alone.
Don't hope to hinder him,
Or to bewilder him.
Sure he's a pilgrim
From the Blarney Stone."

## TRAVELLING TO BLARNEY IN THE GOLDEN AGE OF STEAM ENGINES:

To-day's visitors, arriving at Blarney by coach or by car, might look back with a sense of nostalgia to the days when it was possible to travel out from Cork in a little steam train that puffed its way amid gentle hills and sparkling streams. This service was provided by the Cork and Muskerry Light Railway from 1887 to 1934, In world terms, the whole modern tourist industry was inaugurated by the railway in the nineteenth century, allowing people to travel not only for business but for leisure, and to do so cheaply, quickly and over long distances. The world was on the move and the sights of Europe were all within a day's journey. The railway brought Killarney and Blarney within everyone's reach. The Irish railway companies were advertising tourist tickets in conjunction with the

English railways and the cross-channel steamers. These developments reached their peak when wealthy Americans started the fashion of coming to Europe in search of cultural enrichment, crossing the Atlantic in the great luxury liners, the queens of the ocean. The port of Cork was the first European port of call after the long voyage, and the Americans kept on coming, eager to see the Emerald Isle, to trace their ancestors, to be enchanted by the remains of a long and heroic past. Two things had to be accomplished before heading for Dublin, the Blarney Stone had to be kissed, and the Lakes of Killarney had to be viewed in all their shimmering loveliness. The way to get there was by train. The promoters of the Muskerry Light Railway consciously aimed at the tourist trade to Blarney Castle, as well as providing a service for the everyday business of the local community. They rented a portion of the Castle grounds from the owner, Sir George Colthurst, to provide a station immediately outside the present entrance gates. The Colthurst and Jefferyes families intermarried in 1846. The Cork city terminal was at the site of the present Jury's Hotel on the Western Road. The train ran along the public road. Old photographs show the Blarney train with a fine head of steam as it passes a city tram. The service began on Monday, the 8th of August, 1887, and on the following Sunday almost two thousand passengers were carried on excursion trains to a sports meeting at Blarney. There was quite a lucrative trade in first class passengers alighting at St. Anne's stop to attend the Health Resort or Hydropathic Institution which had been established in 1848 by a Dr. Barter. With increased demand the railway was in due course extended to Coachford and Donoughmore. The exact speed attained by the Blarney train had been the subject of intense debate over many a pint in many a Cork pub! One regular schoolboy passenger, who ended his career as a Catholic bishop in Honolulu, recalled that he thought the train was going quite fast until he looked out the window and saw it being overtaken by a donkey and cart at full trot! And it may not be altogether a myth that every September the following notice appeared in the carriages: "Passengers are requested not to pick blackberries while the train is in motion!" But the much-loved little railway suffered the fate of so many others of its kind and was beaten out of existence by the competition of road transport. The last train steamed bravely out from Cork on Saturday, the 29th of December 1934.

These pages have told something of the story of Blarney Castle over the long span of five hundred years of living and loving and fighting, of the rise and fall of ancestral chiefs, of landlords who made industries beside running waters, and of men and women who waters, and of men and women who made fine cloth. Something of the charm of Blarney comes from recalling the lives of those people and from visiting the places where their memories linger. That alone would be a memorable experience. But the great memorial of all that historic past is Blarney Castle itself, splendid in its antiquity, yet kept fresh and warm by the laughter of those who cross the world to Kiss the Blarney Stone.

# GUIDED TOUR TO CASTLE AND GROUNDS

1. **Entrance Gate**
The view from the Entrance Gate sets the scene immediately, with fine vistas of parkland crowned by Blarney Castle rising up in all its ancient splendour, framed by clumps of trees. The natural setting, so tranquil and so green, is enhanced by the sight and sound of water, as the little river Martin flows alongside the path. Even before reaching the Castle the visitor will have met three rivers, as the Martin joins the Shournagh and the Blarney.

The Blarney Castle Estate consists of 1,130 acres, of which 730 acres are laid out in forest plantations, while there are 400 acres of avenues and parklands. Blarney Lake has $22^1/_2$ acres of water. So there is a feast of natural beauty to be enjoyed, especially the trees, yew, oak, pine and beech, together with rare shrubs and a variety of bird life, and a herd of deer.

## 2. Looking at Blarney Castle

Pause here just to look at Blarney Castle and to appreciate the size and the strength of that enormous pile of stonework that has withstood the ravages of war, weather and time for over five hundred years. The immediate impression is one of massive strength and durability, and the imagination wanders back in time to the stonemasons and the labourers who built it at a time when every stone had to be manipulated by sheer human strength. The mammoth work of construction was begun in 1446 by Cormac MacCarthy, King of Munster, whose prowess as a warrior was proclaimed in the Irish language name given to him by his contemporaries, Cormac Laidir, Cormac the Strong.

He wanted a fortress sufficiently splendid to mark his superiority over the surrounding Munster chiefs, and sufficiently strong to guarantee safety against attack.

The last thing he had in mind was the building of a tourist attraction! A castle was a strategic military building, and the first consideration had to be the location of the site. Castles were always built on an elevated site in order to give a clear view of the surrounding countryside form all points north, south, east and west. This was a vital necessity to give the defenders n early warning of approaching danger. Everything outside and inside a castle was designed to give protection in that supreme hour of crisis when the enemy appeared outside the walls. Blarney Castle is built on an elevated outcrop of solid limestone rock, sufficiently strong to give a firm foundation to the massive pile of stonework. The walls at the base are 18 feet thick to withstand any attempt to break through, the slit windows on the upper portions would stop arrows or stones penetrating inside; the battlements at the top allowed the defenders to pour boiling water, tar and stones down on the heads of the enemy at ground level. The stump of a outer guard tower stands to the left. Such towers were found at intervals in the original defence walls which enclosed the Castle compound, reputed to cover eight acres, and of which the present square tower, or keep, was the centrepiece.

3. **Ground level**
   **Openings** Directly ahead at ground level are three openings, with the one on the right being the Dog Kennel, where

the faithful hound performed a task still valued by all of us to-day, he barked to alert the sentries to the presence of strangers. In the centre is the Sentry Box, where a rotation of armed guards did duty by day and night. On the left is the entrance to the Dungeon, but there is some disagreement about whether or not prisoners were kept here. What is certain is that here was the Castle well, a vital amenity for everyday living, and so needing to be safely enclosed and to be accessible even if the Castle was under siege. So a tower was built around and above it, with steps leading up to the main courtyard. This tower has long been closed off.

Stand back from these three openings and look to the extreme right where a low natural cavern appears in the rock. For anyone anxious to walk backwards into primitive time this is the place to go, for it was certainly there long before Blarney Castle was built, and is probably prehistoric. It leads to a fine view of Blarney Lake. But the eager visitor must be warned to be sure of possessing certain attributes before attempting to explore it, such qualities as a very bendable back, the eyes of a cat, and a sublime indifference to ever again seeing the light of day! Follow the arrows to the left which will shortly lead to the entrance to the Castle. Looking to the right, the ruins of a late eighteenth century mansion will be seen. This was built by the Jeffereys family who had bought the Blarney Estate in 1703 and found the Castle to be decidedly uncomfortable and damp as a family residence. It was accidently destroyed by fire in 1820. Take note that down to the left is the Rock Close which will be well worth a visit when the tour of the Castle is completed.

4. **Stepping into Blarney Castle**

Passing through the great iron gateway with its interlaced bars, the visitor now has the historic experience of stepping into Blarney Castle, the most famous of all the castles of Ireland. Everything to be seen bears the mark of a long tradition and of a lifestyle so utterly different from that of to-day. Therein lies its appeal to the imagination, the power that makes us pause and wonder at sights at once so strange and so intriguing . . . Such romantic thoughts, however, were not in the minds of the men who designed and built this massive pile of stone. They created a building that followed sound architectural principles, that was compact in its use of space, and that met the one essential consideration, to give protection to the MacCarthy family and garrison within in time of attack or siege. Two features in this small entrance lobby illustrate that point, firstly the spyhole through which all visitors could be scrutinised from within. More deadly is the "Murder Hole" overhead; the stone slab when removed left an opening through which an undesirable intruder could be attacked with a pike or sword or with boiling tar or water.

## 5. Large Ground Floor
**Room**  Basically, there are five storeys, each containing a main living area and numerous smaller chambers, alcoves and connecting passages. This ground floor room, measuring 39 feet by 15 feet, had a wooden ceiling as is indicated by the existing stone corbels embedded in the walls. Portion of it was probably used for the reception of supplies, while a partitioned section would provide sleeping quarters for young men and warriors. The floor would have been strewn with rushes on which the men would have stretched out at night, wrapped in their great cloaks. Such refinements as beds, private rooms, bathroom facilities, were certainly not standard equipment in any castle. Because this room was at ground level it would be dangerous to have any wide opening in the walls, hence there is only one slit window.

6. **Great Hall** This fine chamber with its vaulted roof and splendid fireplace was the great Hall, the nerve-centre of the everyday life of the Castle. Here the lord and lady received their honoured guests with ceremonial state; the walls echoed to the sound of excited talk and happy laughter; in the days when the only news was that brought by the latest guest to arrive on horseback, here many a tale was told of happenings great and small in the big world beyond the hills, the politics of the day, the news from Dublin, from London, from Rome, the military adventures of other Munster chiefs, the deaths, the births, the marriages, the secrets, the scandals, the speculations, all of these were here discussed by men and women who spoke in Irish and for whom this Great Hall was the centre of the world.

The splendid fireplace was undoubtedly a matter of favourable comment; originally castles did not have such a luxury, and a fire of logs was placed on the stone floor

in the centre of the room. It
certainly gave heat, but it also gave
smoke which billowed all around,
hurting people's eyes and making
them cough. Fortunately, the lady
of the house was not worried about
the wallpaper or the curtains, for
again such luxuries were not found
even in the most exalted of noble
dwellings. Chimney pieces,
fireplaces and flues to take the
smoke upwards to the sky were
becoming the latest craze in
domestic comfort in Elizabethan
times. The Great Hall was sparsely
furnished; there were rushes on the
floor which the servants changed
when important guests were
expected. After all, even the Lord
of Blarney had a mother-in-law! The
walls were sturdy but they were
damp, and the bare stonework
looked harsh. Squares of tapestry
were hung on them, and it was only
when someone got the bright idea of
taking the tapestries off the walls
and laying them on the floor that the
Great Age of Carpet was invented.
The furniture did little for bodily
comfort; the best seat was the
lord's great oak chair, a chair of
state in which he presided over
councils of state and convivial
occasions. Most of the other
seating consisted of long oak
forms, oak tables, oak side chests.
Lighting came from rush torches set
in the walls, throwing a mellow glow
on a game of chess, or a lively
dance, or a night of talk made
festive by Spanish wine and Irish
whiskey.

## 7. The Earl's Bedroom

Privacy was not something provided for in any castle, especially the privacy of a separate bedroom. The Earl's bedroom, therefore, was a major feature of domestic convenience. Because it was so high up from the outside ground level it could safely afford the luxury of numerous windows, and so was the best-lit room in the whole Castle. Its projecting oriel window could be seen on the outside from the surrounding countryside, and from within its three lights and two side lights offered panoramic views. In addition there is a smaller window facing west, plus two tiny windows facing south. So the Earl had a highly desirable view covering all points north, south, east and west. He needed that not just to admire the sunset but to keep a sharp lookout for any possible danger. He and his lady would have shared a four-poster bed, protected from draughts by a canopy, but there was little else in the line of comfort or embellishment. Morning ablutions were performed from earthenware or pewter jugs and basins, with hot water brought by servants from the kitchen. The present-day preoccupation with personal hygiene, with baths and showers and sanitation, was unknown: Queen Elizabeth had black teeth because she was very fond of sweets but never brushed her teeth. Yet she was so fashion conscious that she had over three hundred dresses in the royal wardrobes. It can only be hoped that the relative rigours of the Earl's Bedroom were mitigated by soft words and sweet dreams.

8. **Young Ladies Bedroom**

On returning to the stairs, a turn to the right leads to a small chamber known as the Garderobe or toilet for overnight use. The night vessels would be emptied by the servants each morning. A few steps upwards lead to the Young Ladies Room, measuring 13 feet by 14 1/2 feet, and with four slit windows. In the masculine world of castle life the young ladies were groomed for the only career open to them, to become young brides of future lords and eventually mistresses of other Irish castles. The other choice was to enter a convent. The young ladies were educated at home by a governess, learning Irish and possibly Latin, and acquiring the social graces of ladylike development, skill at fancy needlework, and the ability to dance, to sing and to play a musical instrument. It was of such things, spiced by speculation on the amorous qualities of certain young knights, that the young ladies spoke of here in this chamber perched high on the walls of Blarney Castle.

9. **The Family Room**

The corridor from the Young Ladies Room leads to the Family Room, measuring $36^{1}/_{2}$ feet by 15 feet, and having four windows, one with three lights, two with two lights, and one slit window. With so much darkness in the stairways and passages, it must have been refreshing for the family to gather in this chamber. The massive fireplace opening tells of warm gatherings and homely talk around a blazing log fire. As regards comforts it was again a matter of rushes on the floor and oak chairs, with candles and torches to light the darkness of long winter evenings.

## 10. The Banqueting Hall

Having left the Family Room through the corridor called the Mural Room, derived from the Latin word, murus, meaning a wall, the stairs leads up to the Banqueting Hall, the heart of the social life of the Castle. Feasting was a way of life in every castle, combining the modern pattern of evening dinner with a whole night's entertainment. An elaborate series of courses was served, fish, eggs, fowl, roast meat, all the meats were highly spiced to keep them fresh. And so a plentiful supply of drink was on hand, mead, beer, wine, whiskey. It must be realised that such modern beverages as tea and coffee were not available, so that even the children were drinking beer at their mother's knee. And nobody bothered about their waistlines. Seated on his great chair at the top of the long oak table, the lord presided at the banquet with aplomb. The high ranks sat around him "above the salt"; the lower sat "below the salt." The castle steward supervised the serving, ensuring that all were served with a ceremonial befitting their rank. To serve at the lord's table was a privilege much coveted by the teenage boys known as pages. It was the custom for noblemen to send their sons of six or seven years to be fostered, or reared, at other castles, so that they would not be spoiled by soft rearing at home. In their new homes the boys got a tough training for their future careers as fighting men. But they were also schooled in courtly manners, and serving at the lord's table was deemed essential to the education of a young gentleman and future knight. Serving dishes and drinking goblets were made of pewter. As the meal progressed the lord's personal bard would provide entertainment by plucking his harp strings and singing songs that celebrated the ancestral prowess of the MacCarthy clan.

**11. The Chapel**

The final upstairs domestic chamber was the Castle Chapel. Here the household gathered for Mass said in Latin, while the chaplain also acted as tutor to the younger members of the family. The builder of Blarney Castle, Cormac Laidir MacCarthy, was a generous patron of the Church and built five churches, including Kilcrea Abbey where he was buried, and which became the traditional burial place of the lords of Blarney.

12. **Up to the Battlements and the Blarney Stone**
The first thing to do on the battlements is to pause to admire the panoramic view of lush, green countryside that stretches out to the north, south, east and west. From this point the visitor, like the ancient lords of Blarney, is monarch of all that he surveys. The strategic military advantage of a castle on the hill will now be fully appreciated, as all approaches to Blarney Castle came under the scrutiny of the sentries on duty here on the battlements. In architectural terms the Castle is described as having machicolated battlements, referring to the fringe of stonework which is built out from the walls on all four sides, supported by stone joists known as corbels. Observe the slits so formed to allow the defenders to shoot arrows and pour boiling liquids down on the attackers at the base of the Castle.

Note, too, the shape of the heavy stone flags that line the walkway around the battlements; they have an apex shape to allow for drainage of water on all four sides. Of course, the highlight of the visit to the battlements is the ritual of Kissing the Blarney Stone to be forever endowed with the gift of Irish eloquence. Any attempt to put that traditional ritual into mere words would be a vulgar intrusion into an experience shrouded in mystery, sweetened by romance, and sustained by the belief of the tens of thousands of people from all over the world who have come to this ancient place to perform that one act.

## 13. Coming down to earth and into the Kitchen

Beginning to descend the narrow stairs brings home the point of why the stairs was designed to be just so narrow. Once again, it was a matter of defence. In the event of the enemy gaining access to the Castle, only one attacker could advance up the stairs, and he could effectively be dealt with by the defender wielding an axe or sword. This wounded or dead figure would fall back on his companions further down the stairs, so allowing the defender to force the enemy to retreat downwards. And in this desperate encounter on the narrow stairs, the defender had the enormous advantage of height. The Kitchen was placed adjacent to the Banqueting Hall for reasons of obvious convenience, but there was also the consideration that having it to high up in the building reduced the risk of having the Castle destroyed by fire. Here was a centre of frenzied activity as the steward and the cooks and the young pages concocted the food for the lord and his guests, the air filled with the savoury smells of pies and broths and tarts, of roast duck, roast venison and roast pork, of pigeons, partridges and salmon, all highly spiced. Note the massive chimney shaft, with its memory of the huge log fire and the revolving spit which held the meat to be roasted. It was the task of old men or young boys to stand there and keep the spit revolving slowly, under the watchful eye of the cook. The lord of Blarney did not want his dinner burnt to cinders!

## 14. The Rock Close

Now it is time for fresh air and a relaxing stroll beneath the great yew trees in the Rock Close. Apart altogether from historical associations, this is an enchanting place, restful to the mind, and unspoilt in its natural beauty. And the long shadow of time is here, too, for even Blarney Castle is modern in comparison with the history of this secluded spot. The massive rock formations and the great boulders indicate that in pre-historic times it was a Druidic settlement or place of worship. The druids were the priests of the old pagan religion which existed in Ireland before the coming of St. Patrick in 432, and they worshipped the Sun God. A leisurely walk around will reveal the Druid's Altar, the Witch's Kitchen, and the Wishing Steps, which have to be traversed downwards and upwards with closed eyes to have one's wish to come true. Most of the curious rocks stand to-day as they have stood for over two thousand years, though some arrangements were man made by the Jeffereys family in the late eighteenth century.

The variety and splendour of the trees bring added interest, ancient yew and ilex, with the yew tree over the Witch's Kitchen being judged by experts to be over a thousand years old. Other specimen trees are California redwood, incense cedar, cypress and thuya, beech and rare varieties of oak. All of this natural beauty, offset by running water and rustic bridges, gives the Rock Close something of the enchantment of a fairy glade.

15. **Blarney House** **Castle**
The spires of Blarney Castle House beckon the visitor to stroll across the parkland to see the elegant

interior of a period country house. The experience will not only be an intriguing contrast to what has just been seen at Blarney Castle,

but will lead to an appreciation of fine craftsmanship and of the lifestyle of an age when a sense of beauty made for gracious living. The visitor will be taken on a conducted tour.

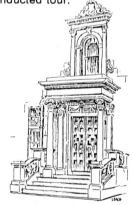

### 16. Blarney Village

Blarney village is one of the finest examples in Ireland of the creation of a model estate village, and will provide an interesting and relaxing end to the Blarney experience. The full story of how the village was created as an outcrop of the Blarney Castle Estate in the late eighteenth century has already been told, but now is the time to walk around and see the reality.